YEAR
TEAM

PAGE 01

NAME

AGE

HEIGHT

WEIGHT

POSITION

SHOOT/GLOVE HAND

NUMBER

COACH

ASSISTANT COACH

MANAGER

TRAINER

HOME ARENA

INSERT TEAM PHOTO HERE

PLAYERS IN BACK ROW

PLAYERS IN MIDDLE ROW

PLAYERS IN FRONT ROW

YEAR | PAGE 02

DIVISION
LEAGUE

TEAMS

1		7
2		8
3		9
4		10
5		11
6		12

EXHIBITION GAMES

NO	DATE MM/DD	OPPONENT	SCORE US	SCORE OPP	W	L	T	TEAM PTS	GOALIE	GA	G	A	PM	PTS	+/-	G	A	PM	PTS	+/-
01																				
02																				
03																				
04																				
05																				
06																				
07																				
08																				
09																				
10																				

Columns: TEAM (SCORE, TEAM RECORD, GOALIE, GA) | PERSONAL (POINTS, TOTALS)

REGULAR SEASON GAMES

NO	DATE MM/DD	OPPONENT	SCORE US	SCORE OPP	W	L	T	TEAM PTS	GOALIE	GA	G	A	PM	PTS	+/-	G	A	PM	PTS	+/-
01																				
02																				
03																				
04																				
05																				
06																				
07																				
08																				
09																				
10																				

Quickfact: Did you know that, according to reliefs found in Greece, one of the earliest forms of hockey was played in ancient Greece about 500 B.C.?

REGULAR SEASON GAMES

YEAR

PAGE 03

NO	DATE MM/DD	OPPONENT	SCORE US	SCORE OPP	TEAM RECORD W	TEAM RECORD L	TEAM RECORD T	TEAM PTS	GOALIE	GA	POINTS G	A	PM	PTS	+/-	TOTALS G	A	PM	PTS	+/-
11																				
12																				
13																				
14																				
15																				
16																				
17																				
18																				
19																				
20																				
21																				
22																				
23																				
24																				
25																				
26																				
27																				
28																				
29																				
30																				
31																				
32																				
33																				
34																				
35																				
36																				
37																				
38																				
39																				
40																				
41																				
42																				
43																				
44																				
45																				
46																				
47																				
48																				
49																				
50																				
51																				

SEASON TOTALS

TEAM

GAMES	W	L	PTS	+/-

GOALIE

GAMES	GAA

PERSONAL

GAMES	W	L	PTS	+/-

Quickfact: Did you know that a hockey puck weighs about six ounces (170 gm)?

YEAR

FINAL STANDINGS

1.
2.
3.
4.
5.
6.
7.
8.
9.
10.
11.
12.

QUICK TIPS

- ☑ Get yourself into a positive state of mind before each game!
- ☑ Start each game strong and finish each game strong!
- ☑ Think about your best performances and victories!
- ☑ It's the thought of defeat that causes defeat.
- ☑ Concentrate on what you are doing and you will succeed!
- ☑ Relax, stay loose, do your best and most importantly, HAVE FUN!

Quickfact: Did you know that the size of an official NHL size rink is 200 feet (60.8 m) long and 85 feet (25.8 m) wide?

YEAR

PLAYOFFS

PAGE 05

SERIES 1

NO	DATE MM/DD	OPPONENT	TEAM SCORE US	OPP	SERIES RECORD W	L	T	W	L	T	TOTAL PTS	GOALIE	GA	PERSONAL POINTS G	A	PM	PTS	+/-	TOTALS G	A	PM	PTS	+/-
01																							
02																							
03																							
04																							
05																							
06																							
07																							

SERIES 2

NO	DATE MM/DD	OPPONENT	TEAM SCORE US	OPP	SERIES RECORD W	L	T	W	L	T	TOTAL PTS	GOALIE	GA	PERSONAL POINTS G	A	PM	PTS	+/-	TOTALS G	A	PM	PTS	+/-
01																							
02																							
03																							
04																							
05																							
06																							
07																							

SERIES 3

NO	DATE MM/DD	OPPONENT	TEAM SCORE US	OPP	SERIES RECORD W	L	T	W	L	T	TOTAL PTS	GOALIE	GA	PERSONAL POINTS G	A	PM	PTS	+/-	TOTALS G	A	PM	PTS	+/-
01																							
02																							
03																							
04																							
05																							
06																							
07																							

FINAL STANDINGS: _____

COMMENTS: _____

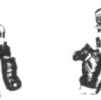

_____

_____

_____

Quickfact: Did you know that the size of an official European rink is 13.3 feet (4m) wider and 13.3 feet (4m) longer than the NHL rink?

TOURNAMENTS

YEAR

PAGE 06

TOURNAMENT NAME — DATE

NO	DATE MM/DD	OPPONENT	SCORE US	SCORE OPP	W	L	T	TEAM PTS	GOALIE	GA	G	A	PM	PTS	+/-	G	A	PM	PTS	+/-
01																				
02																				
03																				
04																				
05																				
06																				
07																				

Columns grouped under: TEAM RECORD, PERSONAL RECORDS (POINTS, TOTALS)

RESULTS:

TOURNAMENT NAME — DATE

NO	DATE MM/DD	OPPONENT	SCORE US	SCORE OPP	W	L	T	TEAM PTS	GOALIE	GA	G	A	PM	PTS	+/-	G	A	PM	PTS	+/-
01																				
02																				
03																				
04																				
05																				
06																				
07																				

RESULTS:

TOURNAMENT NAME — DATE

NO	DATE MM/DD	OPPONENT	SCORE US	SCORE OPP	W	L	T	TEAM PTS	GOALIE	GA	G	A	PM	PTS	+/-	G	A	PM	PTS	+/-
01																				
02																				
03																				
04																				
05																				
06																				
07																				

RESULTS:

Quickfact: Did you know that Jacques Plante was the first goalie to wear a mask in a regular-season game in the NHL on November 1, 1959 after being hit in the face by a shot by Andy Bathgate?

HOCKEY STORIES

YEAR

PAGE 07

AWARDS AND ACHIEVEMENTS:

MEMORABLE PLAYS:

FUNNY MOMENTS:

Quickfact: Did you know that in 1955 the NHL started putting the crest of the home team on the puck?

YEAR
TEAM

PAGE 08

NAME

AGE

HEIGHT

WEIGHT

POSITION

SHOOT/GLOVE HAND

NUMBER

COACH

ASSISTANT COACH

MANAGER

TRAINER

HOME ARENA

INSERT TEAM PHOTO HERE

PLAYERS IN BACK ROW

PLAYERS IN MIDDLE ROW

PLAYERS IN FRONT ROW

YEAR **PAGE 09**

DIVISION
LEAGUE

TEAMS

#	Team	#	Team
1		7	
2		8	
3		9	
4		10	
5		11	
6		12	

EXHIBITION GAMES

NO	DATE MM/DD	OPPONENT	SCORE US	SCORE OPP	W	L	T	TEAM PTS	GOALIE	GA	G	A	PM	PTS	+/-	G	A	PM	PTS	+/-
01																				
02																				
03																				
04																				
05																				
06																				
07																				
08																				
09																				
10																				

TEAM / PERSONAL — POINTS / TOTALS

REGULAR SEASON GAMES

NO	DATE MM/DD	OPPONENT	SCORE US	SCORE OPP	W	L	T	TEAM PTS	GOALIE	GA	G	A	PM	PTS	+/-	G	A	PM	PTS	+/-
01																				
02																				
03																				
04																				
05																				
06																				
07																				
08																				
09																				
10																				

Quickfact: Did you know that all NHL rinks were flooded and scraped using zambonis by 1955-56?

YEAR

REGULAR SEASON GAMES

PAGE 10

NO	DATE MM/DD	OPPONENT	SCORE US	SCORE OPP	TEAM RECORD W	TEAM RECORD L	TEAM RECORD T	TEAM PTS	GOALIE	GA	G	A	PM	PTS	+/-	G	A	PM	PTS	+/-
11																				
12																				
13																				
14																				
15																				
16																				
17																				
18																				
19																				
20																				
21																				
22																				
23																				
24																				
25																				
26																				
27																				
28																				
29																				
30																				
31																				
32																				
33																				
34																				
35																				
36																				
37																				
38																				
39																				
40																				
41																				
42																				
43																				
44																				
45																				
46																				
47																				
48																				
49																				
50																				
51																				

SEASON TOTALS

TEAM

GAMES	W	L	PTS	+/-

GOALIE

GAMES	GAA

PERSONAL

GAMES	W	L	PTS	+/-

Quickfact: Did you know that a hockey puck is made of vulcanized rubber and is about 1" (2.5 cm) and 3" (7.6 cm) in diameter?

FINAL STANDINGS

1.
2.
3.
4.
5.
6.
7.
8.
9.
10.
11.
12.

QUICK TIPS

- ☑ Self-motivation, self-preparation, self-discipline, self-dedication are important ingredients for winners!
- ☑ Draw positive energy from the environment!
- ☑ Don't overreact to bad calls by referees!
- ☑ Be mentally prepared to play!
- ☑ Be in top physical condition!
- ☑ Correct your mistakes next shift!

Quickfact: Did you know that the maximum allowable curve on a hockey stick is 1/2 inch (1.27 cm)?

PLAYOFFS

YEAR

PAGE 12

SERIES 1

NO	DATE MM/DD	OPPONENT	SCORE US	SCORE OPP	W	L	T	SERIES RECORD W	SERIES RECORD L	SERIES RECORD T	TOTAL PTS	GOALIE	GA	POINTS G	A	PM	PTS	+/-	TOTALS G	A	PM	PTS	+/-
01																							
02																							
03																							
04																							
05																							
06																							
07																							

SERIES 2

NO	DATE MM/DD	OPPONENT	SCORE US	SCORE OPP	W	L	T	SERIES RECORD W	SERIES RECORD L	SERIES RECORD T	TOTAL PTS	GOALIE	GA	POINTS G	A	PM	PTS	+/-	TOTALS G	A	PM	PTS	+/-
01																							
02																							
03																							
04																							
05																							
06																							
07																							

SERIES 3

NO	DATE MM/DD	OPPONENT	SCORE US	SCORE OPP	W	L	T	SERIES RECORD W	SERIES RECORD L	SERIES RECORD T	TOTAL PTS	GOALIE	GA	POINTS G	A	PM	PTS	+/-	TOTALS G	A	PM	PTS	+/-
01																							
02																							
03																							
04																							
05																							
06																							
07																							

FINAL STANDINGS: _____

COMMENTS: _____
_____
_____

Quickfact: Did you know that the angle made by the shaft of the stick and the blade is called the lie?

YEAR / PAGE 13

TOURNAMENTS

TOURNAMENT NAME — DATE

NO	DATE MM/DD	OPPONENT	SCORE US	SCORE OPP	W	L	T	TEAM PTS	GOALIE	GA	G	A	PM	PTS	+/-	G	A	PM	PTS	+/-
01																				
02																				
03																				
04																				
05																				
06																				
07																				

Columns grouped as: SCORE (US/OPP), TEAM RECORD (W/L/T/TEAM PTS), GOALIE, GA, PERSONAL RECORDS — POINTS (G/A/PM/PTS/+/-), TOTALS (G/A/PM/PTS/+/-)

RESULTS:

TOURNAMENT NAME — DATE

NO	DATE MM/DD	OPPONENT	SCORE US	SCORE OPP	W	L	T	TEAM PTS	GOALIE	GA	G	A	PM	PTS	+/-	G	A	PM	PTS	+/-
01																				
02																				
03																				
04																				
05																				
06																				
07																				

RESULTS:

TOURNAMENT NAME — DATE

NO	DATE MM/DD	OPPONENT	SCORE US	SCORE OPP	W	L	T	TEAM PTS	GOALIE	GA	G	A	PM	PTS	+/-	G	A	PM	PTS	+/-
01																				
02																				
03																				
04																				
05																				
06																				
07																				

RESULTS:

Quickfact: Did you know that pucks are frozen before a game to reduce their bounce on the ice surface?

YEAR

HOCKEY STORIES

PAGE 14

AWARDS AND ACHIEVEMENTS:

MEMORABLE PLAYS:

FUNNY MOMENTS:

🏒 **Quickfact:** Did you know that the linesman places the puck on the ice during time-outs or TV breaks to prevent the puck from warming up and causing undue bouncing?

YEAR

TEAM

PAGE 15

NAME

AGE

HEIGHT

WEIGHT

POSITION

SHOOT/GLOVE HAND

NUMBER

COACH

ASSISTANT COACH

MANAGER

TRAINER

HOME ARENA

INSERT TEAM PHOTO HERE

PLAYERS IN BACK ROW

PLAYERS IN MIDDLE ROW

PLAYERS IN FRONT ROW

YEAR | PAGE 16

DIVISION LEAGUE

TEAMS

1		7
2		8
3		9
4		10
5		11
6		12

EXHIBITION GAMES

NO	DATE	OPPONENT	SCORE		TEAM RECORD				GOALIE	GA	POINTS					TOTALS				
	MM/DD		US	OPP	W	L	T	TEAM PTS			G	A	PM	PTS	+/-	G	A	PM	PTS	+/-
01																				
02																				
03																				
04																				
05																				
06																				
07																				
08																				
09																				
10																				

REGULAR SEASON GAMES

NO	DATE	OPPONENT	SCORE		TEAM RECORD				GOALIE	GA	POINTS					TOTALS				
	MM/DD		US	OPP	W	L	T	TEAM PTS			G	A	PM	PTS	+/-	G	A	PM	PTS	+/-
01																				
02																				
03																				
04																				
05																				
06																				
07																				
08																				
09																				
10																				

Quickfact: Did you know that the goal posts of a hockey net are 4 feet (1.2 m) high above the ice surface and 6 feet (1.8 m) apart measured from the inside of the posts?

REGULAR SEASON GAMES

YEAR:
PAGE: 17

TEAM | PERSONAL

NO	DATE MM/DD	OPPONENT	SCORE US	SCORE OPP	W	L	T	TEAM PTS	GOALIE	GA	G	A	PM	PTS	+/-	G	A	PM	PTS	+/-
11																				
12																				
13																				
14																				
15																				
16																				
17																				
18																				
19																				
20																				
21																				
22																				
23																				
24																				
25																				
26																				
27																				
28																				
29																				
30																				
31																				
32																				
33																				
34																				
35																				
36																				
37																				
38																				
39																				
40																				
41																				
42																				
43																				
44																				
45																				
46																				
47																				
48																				
49																				
50																				
51																				

SEASON TOTALS

TEAM

GAMES	W	L	PTS	+/-

GOALIE

GAMES	GAA

PERSONAL

GAMES	W	L	PTS	+/-

Quickfact: Did you know that the boards of a rink are between 40 inches (101.6 cm) and 48 inches (121.9 cm) high?

FINAL STANDINGS

1.
2.
3.
4.
5.
6.
7.
8.
9.
10.
11.
12.

QUICK TIPS

- ☑ A player needs concentrated effort to reach any goal.

- ☑ Learn to transfer energy from something negative to something positive!

- ☑ In tough situations and pressure situations, stick to the game plan!

- ☑ Be persistent and determined to win!

- ☑ Make sure that your equipment is in ready form before each game!

- ☑ Always bring an extra stick to each game!

Quickfact: Did you know that the corners of a rink are rounded in the arc of a circle with a radius of about 28 feet (8.5 m)?

PLAYOFFS

YEAR
PAGE 19

SERIES 1

NO	DATE MM/DD	OPPONENT	SCORE US	SCORE OPP	W	L	T	SERIES RECORD W	L	T	TOTAL PTS	GOALIE	GA	POINTS G	A	PM	PTS	+/-	TOTALS G	A	PM	PTS	+/-
01																							
02																								
03																								
04																								
05																								
06																								
07																								

SERIES 2

NO	DATE MM/DD	OPPONENT	SCORE US	SCORE OPP	W	L	T	SERIES RECORD W	L	T	TOTAL PTS	GOALIE	GA	POINTS G	A	PM	PTS	+/-	TOTALS G	A	PM	PTS	+/-
01																								
02																								
03																								
04																								
05																								
06																								
07																								

SERIES 3

NO	DATE MM/DD	OPPONENT	SCORE US	SCORE OPP	W	L	T	SERIES RECORD W	L	T	TOTAL PTS	GOALIE	GA	POINTS G	A	PM	PTS	+/-	TOTALS G	A	PM	PTS	+/-
01																								
02																								
03																								
04																								
05																								
06																								
07																								

FINAL STANDINGS: _____

COMMENTS: _____

_____

_____

_____

Quickfact: Did you know that the number on the back of a NHL jersey is about 10 inches (25.4 cm) high and the name is 3 inches (7.65 cm) high in block letters across the back?

TOURNAMENTS

YEAR

PAGE 20

TOURNAMENT NAME — DATE

NO	DATE MM/DD	OPPONENT	SCORE US / OPP	TEAM RECORD W / L / T / TEAM PTS	GOALIE	GA	POINTS G / A / PM / PTS / +/-	TOTALS G / A / PM / PTS / +/-
01								
02								
03								
04								
05								
06								
07								

PERSONAL RECORDS

RESULTS:

TOURNAMENT NAME — DATE

NO	DATE MM/DD	OPPONENT	SCORE US / OPP	TEAM RECORD W / L / T / TEAM PTS	GOALIE	GA	POINTS G / A / PM / PTS / +/-	TOTALS G / A / PM / PTS / +/-
01								
02								
03								
04								
05								
06								
07								

PERSONAL RECORDS

RESULTS:

TOURNAMENT NAME — DATE

NO	DATE MM/DD	OPPONENT	SCORE US / OPP	TEAM RECORD W / L / T / TEAM PTS	GOALIE	GA	POINTS G / A / PM / PTS / +/-	TOTALS G / A / PM / PTS / +/-
01								
02								
03								
04								
05								
06								
07								

PERSONAL RECORDS

RESULTS:

Quickfact: Did you know that the NHL was formed in 1917?

YEAR

HOCKEY STORIES

PAGE
21

AWARDS AND ACHIEVEMENTS:

MEMORABLE PLAYS:

FUNNY MOMENTS:

Quickfact: Did you know that the hardest shot in the NHL is over 100 miles (160.9 km) per hour?

YEAR

TEAM

PAGE 22

NAME

AGE

HEIGHT

WEIGHT

POSITION

SHOOT/GLOVE HAND

NUMBER

COACH

ASSISTANT COACH

MANAGER

TRAINER

HOME ARENA

INSERT TEAM PHOTO HERE

PLAYERS IN BACK ROW

PLAYERS IN MIDDLE ROW

PLAYERS IN FRONT ROW

YEAR | PAGE 23

DIVISION LEAGUE

TEAMS

#	Team	#	Team
1		7	
2		8	
3		9	
4		10	
5		11	
6		12	

EXHIBITION GAMES

			TEAM							PERSONAL								
NO	DATE	OPPONENT	SCORE		TEAM RECORD				GOALIE	GA	POINTS					TOTALS		
	MM/DD		US	OPP	W	L	T	TEAM PTS			G	A	PM	PTS	+/-	G	A	PM	PTS	+/-
01																				
02																				
03																				
04																				
05																				
06																				
07																				
08																				
09																				
10																				

REGULAR SEASON GAMES

			TEAM							PERSONAL								
NO	DATE	OPPONENT	SCORE		TEAM RECORD				GOALIE	GA	POINTS					TOTALS		
	MM/DD		US	OPP	W	L	T	TEAM PTS			G	A	PM	PTS	+/-	G	A	PM	PTS	+/-
01																				
02																				
03																				
04																				
05																				
06																				
07																				
08																				
09																				
10																				

Quickfact: Did you know that the Stanley Cup was donated in 1893 by Lord Stanley of Preston, who was Governor-General of Canada from 1888 to 1893?

REGULAR SEASON GAMES

YEAR

PAGE 24

TEAM

NO	DATE MM/DD	OPPONENT	SCORE US	SCORE OPP	TEAM RECORD W	TEAM RECORD L	TEAM RECORD T	TEAM PTS	GOALIE	GA
11										
12										
13										
14										
15										
16										
17										
18										
19										
20										
21										
22										
23										
24										
25										
26										
27										
28										
29										
30										
31										
32										
33										
34										
35										
36										
37										
38										
39										
40										
41										
42										
43										
44										
45										
46										
47										
48										
49										
50										
51										

PERSONAL

POINTS: G | A | PM | PTS | +/-

TOTALS: G | A | PM | PTS | +/-

SEASON TOTALS

TEAM
GAMES	W	L	PTS	+/-

GOALIE
GAMES	GAA

PERSONAL
GAMES	W	L	PTS	+/-

Quickfact: Did you know that the first Stanley Cup was awarded to the Montreal Amateur Association in 1893?

FINAL STANDINGS

1.
2.
3.
4.
5.
6.
7.
8.
9.
10.
11.
12.

QUICK TIPS

- ☑ Do not take cheap shots at opposing players during the game!

- ☑ Know the coach's philosophy!

- ☑ Always give 100% effort!

- ☑ You miss 100% of the shots you don't take!

- ☑ Do not take penalties for retaliation!

- ☑ The difference between good and great is extra effort!

Quickfact: Did you know that rockered blades, used by hockey players, make it easier for players to turn quickly?

PLAYOFFS

YEAR: _____ PAGE: 26

SERIES 1

NO	DATE MM/DD	OPPONENT	SCORE US	SCORE OPP	W	L	T	SERIES RECORD W	L	T	TOTAL PTS	GOALIE	GA	G	A	PM	PTS	+/-	G	A	PM	PTS	+/-
01																							
02																							
03																							
04																							
05																							
06																							
07																							

SERIES 2

NO	DATE MM/DD	OPPONENT	SCORE US	SCORE OPP	W	L	T	SERIES RECORD W	L	T	TOTAL PTS	GOALIE	GA	G	A	PM	PTS	+/-	G	A	PM	PTS	+/-
01																							
02																							
03																							
04																							
05																							
06																							
07																							

SERIES 3

NO	DATE MM/DD	OPPONENT	SCORE US	SCORE OPP	W	L	T	SERIES RECORD W	L	T	TOTAL PTS	GOALIE	GA	G	A	PM	PTS	+/-	G	A	PM	PTS	+/-
01																							
02																							
03																							
04																							
05																							
06																							
07																							

FINAL STANDINGS: _____

COMMENTS: _____
_____
_____
_____

● Quickfact: Did you know that rockering blades creates a gentle curve in the very sharp blade of an ice skate by rounding the toe and heel of the blade?

TOURNAMENTS

YEAR
PAGE 27

TOURNAMENT NAME — DATE

NO	DATE MM/DD	OPPONENT	SCORE US	SCORE OPP	W	L	T	TEAM PTS	GOALIE	GA	G	A	PM	PTS	+/-	G	A	PM	PTS	+/-
01																				
02																				
03																				
04																				
05																				
06																				
07																				

Columns grouped under: TEAM RECORD (W, L, T, TEAM PTS); PERSONAL RECORDS — POINTS (G, A, PM, PTS, +/-); TOTALS (G, A, PM, PTS, +/-)

RESULTS:

TOURNAMENT NAME — DATE

NO	DATE MM/DD	OPPONENT	SCORE US	SCORE OPP	W	L	T	TEAM PTS	GOALIE	GA	G	A	PM	PTS	+/-	G	A	PM	PTS	+/-
01																				
02																				
03																				
04																				
05																				
06																				
07																				

RESULTS:

TOURNAMENT NAME — DATE

NO	DATE MM/DD	OPPONENT	SCORE US	SCORE OPP	W	L	T	TEAM PTS	GOALIE	GA	G	A	PM	PTS	+/-	G	A	PM	PTS	+/-
01																				
02																				
03																				
04																				
05																				
06																				
07																				

RESULTS:

Quickfact: Did you know that in the 1940's the referees first began using hand gestures to signal the penalties that they were calling on the ice?

YEAR | HOCKEY STORIES | PAGE 28

AWARDS AND ACHIEVEMENTS:

MEMORABLE PLAYS:

FUNNY MOMENTS:

Quickfact: In the earliest days of hockey the goal judge stood behind the net and would raise his flag and collect the puck when a goal was scored?

YEAR
TEAM

PAGE 29

NAME

AGE

HEIGHT

WEIGHT

POSITION

SHOOT/GLOVE HAND

NUMBER

COACH

ASSISTANT COACH

MANAGER

TRAINER

HOME ARENA

INSERT TEAM PHOTO HERE

PLAYERS IN BACK ROW

PLAYERS IN MIDDLE ROW

PLAYERS IN FRONT ROW

DIVISION LEAGUE

YEAR

PAGE 30

TEAMS

#	Team	#	Team
1		7	
2		8	
3		9	
4		10	
5		11	
6		12	

EXHIBITION GAMES

			TEAM								PERSONAL							
NO	DATE	OPPONENT	SCORE		TEAM RECORD			GOALIE	GA	POINTS					TOTALS			
	MM/DD		US	OPP	W	L	T	TEAM PTS			G	A	PM	PTS	+/-	G	A	PM	PTS	+/-
01																				
02																				
03																				
04																				
05																				
06																				
07																				
08																				
09																				
10																				

REGULAR SEASON GAMES

			TEAM								PERSONAL							
NO	DATE	OPPONENT	SCORE		TEAM RECORD			GOALIE	GA	POINTS					TOTALS			
	MM/DD		US	OPP	W	L	T	TEAM PTS			G	A	PM	PTS	+/-	G	A	PM	PTS	+/-
01																				
02																				
03																				
04																				
05																				
06																				
07																				
08																				
09																				
10																				

Quickfact: Did you know that around 1919 the west coast teams used "western rules" which included a seventh skater or "rover" ?

REGULAR SEASON GAMES

YEAR

PAGE 31

TEAM | PERSONAL

NO	DATE MM/DD	OPPONENT	SCORE US	SCORE OPP	TEAM RECORD W	L	T	TEAM PTS	GOALIE	GA	POINTS G	A	PM	PTS	+/-	TOTALS G	A	PM	PTS	+/-
11																				
12																				
13																				
14																				
15																				
16																				
17																				
18																				
19																				
20																				
21																				
22																				
23																				
24																				
25																				
26																				
27																				
28																				
29																				
30																				
31																				
32																				
33																				
34																				
35																				
36																				
37																				
38																				
39																				
40																				
41																				
42																				
43																				
44																				
45																				
46																				
47																				
48																				
49																				
50																				
51																				

SEASON TOTALS

TEAM

GAMES	W	L	PTS	+/-

GOALIE

GAMES	GAA

PERSONAL

GAMES	W	L	PTS	+/-

Quickfact: Did you know that players played with a straight blade until the 1960's?

FINAL STANDINGS

1.
2.
3.
4.
5.
6.
7.
8.
9.
10.
11.
12.

QUICK TIPS

- ☑ Do not be a selfish player. The word "TEAM" has no "I" in it!
- ☑ Play hard each shift as if it is your last!
- ☑ Good sportsmanship is always important whether you win or lose!
- ☑ Do not take stupid penalties because it may hurt your team!
- ☑ Always get a good night's rest before a game!
- ☑ Stretching before a game is important to prevent injury!

Quickfact: Did you know that the referee's crease is a semi-circle area, with a 10 foot (25.4 cm) radius, marked in red in front of the timekeeper's bench into which players cannot follow a referee?

PLAYOFFS

YEAR
PAGE 33

SERIES 1

NO	DATE MM/DD	OPPONENT	TEAM SCORE US / OPP	W	L	T	SERIES RECORD W	L	T	TOTAL PTS	GOALIE	GA	PERSONAL POINTS G	A	PM	PTS	+/-	TOTALS G	A	PM	PTS	+/-
01																						
02																						
03																						
04																						
05																						
06																						
07																						

SERIES 2

NO	DATE MM/DD	OPPONENT	TEAM SCORE US / OPP	W	L	T	SERIES RECORD W	L	T	TOTAL PTS	GOALIE	GA	PERSONAL POINTS G	A	PM	PTS	+/-	TOTALS G	A	PM	PTS	+/-
01																						
02																						
03																						
04																						
05																						
06																						
07																						

SERIES 3

NO	DATE MM/DD	OPPONENT	TEAM SCORE US / OPP	W	L	T	SERIES RECORD W	L	T	TOTAL PTS	GOALIE	GA	PERSONAL POINTS G	A	PM	PTS	+/-	TOTALS G	A	PM	PTS	+/-
01																						
02																						
03																						
04																						
05																						
06																						
07																						

FINAL STANDINGS: _____

COMMENTS: _____

_____

_____

_____

Quickfact: Did you know that the Stanley Cup is the oldest trophy for which athletes compete in North America and stands almost three feet (1 m) in height?

TOURNAMENTS

YEAR

PAGE 34

TOURNAMENT NAME — DATE

NO	DATE MM/DD	OPPONENT	SCORE US	SCORE OPP	W	L	T	TEAM PTS	GOALIE	GA	G	A	PM	PTS	+/-	G	A	PM	PTS	+/-
01																				
02																				
03																				
04																				
05																				
06																				
07																				

PERSONAL RECORDS — POINTS / TOTALS

RESULTS:

TOURNAMENT NAME — DATE

NO	DATE MM/DD	OPPONENT	SCORE US	SCORE OPP	W	L	T	TEAM PTS	GOALIE	GA	G	A	PM	PTS	+/-	G	A	PM	PTS	+/-
01																				
02																				
03																				
04																				
05																				
06																				
07																				

RESULTS:

TOURNAMENT NAME — DATE

NO	DATE MM/DD	OPPONENT	SCORE US	SCORE OPP	W	L	T	TEAM PTS	GOALIE	GA	G	A	PM	PTS	+/-	G	A	PM	PTS	+/-
01																				
02																				
03																				
04																				
05																				
06																				
07																				

RESULTS:

Quickfact: Did you know that the original Stanley Cup was known as the Dominion Hockey Challenge Cup and cost 50 guineas which was equivalent to about $50. at the time?

YEAR

HOCKEY STORIES

PAGE 35

AWARDS AND ACHIEVEMENTS:

MEMORABLE PLAYS:

FUNNY MOMENTS:

Quickfact: Did you know that in 1910 the game of hockey was changed from two 30 minute periods to three 20 minute periods?

YEAR
TEAM

PAGE 36

NAME

AGE

HEIGHT

WEIGHT

POSITION

SHOOT/GLOVE HAND

NUMBER

COACH

ASSISTANT COACH

MANAGER

TRAINER

HOME ARENA

INSERT TEAM PHOTO HERE

PLAYERS IN BACK ROW

PLAYERS IN MIDDLE ROW

PLAYERS IN FRONT ROW

DIVISION LEAGUE

YEAR | PAGE 37

TEAMS

#	Team	#	Team
1		7	
2		8	
3		9	
4		10	
5		11	
6		12	

EXHIBITION GAMES

NO	DATE MM/DD	OPPONENT	SCORE US	SCORE OPP	W	L	T	TEAM PTS	GOALIE	GA	G	A	PM	PTS	+/-	G	A	PM	PTS	+/-
01																				
02																				
03																				
04																				
05																				
06																				
07																				
08																				
09																				
10																				

REGULAR SEASON GAMES

NO	DATE MM/DD	OPPONENT	SCORE US	SCORE OPP	W	L	T	TEAM PTS	GOALIE	GA	G	A	PM	PTS	+/-	G	A	PM	PTS	+/-
01																				
02																				
03																				
04																				
05																				
06																				
07																				
08																				
09																				
10																				

Quickfact: Did you know the use of a flat disk to play hockey was the first documented on March 3, 1875 in Montreal?

REGULAR SEASON GAMES

YEAR
PAGE 38

TEAM | PERSONAL

NO	DATE MM/DD	OPPONENT	SCORE US	SCORE OPP	TEAM RECORD W	L	T	TEAM PTS	GOALIE	GA	POINTS G	A	PM	PTS	+/-	TOTALS G	A	PM	PTS	+/-
11																				
12																				
13																				
14																				
15																				
16																				
17																				
18																				
19																				
20																				
21																				
22																				
23																				
24																				
25																				
26																				
27																				
28																				
29																				
30																				
31																				
32																				
33																				
34																				
35																				
36																				
37																				
38																				
39																				
40																				
41																				
42																				
43																				
44																				
45																				
46																				
47																				
48																				
49																				
50																				
51																				

SEASON TOTALS

TEAM

GAMES	W	L	PTS	+/-

GOALIE

GAMES	GAA

PERSONAL

GAMES	W	L	PTS	+/-

Quickfact: Did you know that the first puck was cut out of a rubber ball in 1877?

FINAL STANDINGS

1.
2.
3.
4.
5.
6.
7.
8.
9.
10.
11.
12.

QUICK TIPS

- ☑ You should always compete and play to win!
- ☑ Never give up until the final buzzer!
- ☑ Practice hard as if it is a real game situation!
- ☑ Always encourage your teammates!
- ☑ Always be positive on the bench!
- ☑ Eat a good carbohydrate meal a few hours before a game!

Quickfact: Did you know that the first artificial ice skating rink was installed in Frankfurt, Germany in 1881?

PLAYOFFS

YEAR

PAGE 40

SERIES 1

NO	DATE MM/DD	OPPONENT	SCORE US	SCORE OPP	W	L	T	SERIES RECORD W	L	T	TOTAL PTS	GOALIE	GA	G	A	PM	PTS	+/-	G	A	PM	PTS	+/-
01																							
02																							
03																							
04																							
05																							
06																							
07																							

TEAM / **PERSONAL** — POINTS / TOTALS

SERIES 2

NO	DATE MM/DD	OPPONENT	SCORE US	SCORE OPP	W	L	T	SERIES RECORD W	L	T	TOTAL PTS	GOALIE	GA	G	A	PM	PTS	+/-	G	A	PM	PTS	+/-
01																							
02																							
03																							
04																							
05																							
06																							
07																							

SERIES 3

NO	DATE MM/DD	OPPONENT	SCORE US	SCORE OPP	W	L	T	SERIES RECORD W	L	T	TOTAL PTS	GOALIE	GA	G	A	PM	PTS	+/-	G	A	PM	PTS	+/-
01																							
02																							
03																							
04																							
05																							
06																							
07																							

FINAL STANDINGS: _____

COMMENTS: _____

Quickfact: Did you know that the word hockey comes from the French word hoquet, meaning shepherd's crook, referring to the shape of the stick?

TOURNAMENTS

TOURNAMENT NAME | DATE

NO	DATE MM/DD	OPPONENT	SCORE US	SCORE OPP	W	L	T	TEAM PTS	GOALIE	GA	G	A	PM	PTS	+/-	G	A	PM	PTS	+/-
01																				
02																				
03																				
04																				
05																				
06																				
07																				

Column groups: SCORE | TEAM RECORD | GOALIE | GA | PERSONAL RECORDS (POINTS | TOTALS)

RESULTS:

TOURNAMENT NAME | DATE

NO	DATE MM/DD	OPPONENT	SCORE US	SCORE OPP	W	L	T	TEAM PTS	GOALIE	GA	G	A	PM	PTS	+/-	G	A	PM	PTS	+/-
01																				
02																				
03																				
04																				
05																				
06																				
07																				

RESULTS:

TOURNAMENT NAME | DATE

NO	DATE MM/DD	OPPONENT	SCORE US	SCORE OPP	W	L	T	TEAM PTS	GOALIE	GA	G	A	PM	PTS	+/-	G	A	PM	PTS	+/-
01																				
02																				
03																				
04																				
05																				
06																				
07																				

RESULTS:

Quickfact: Did you know that playing sports, such as hockey, was considered immoral by some in the 19th century?

HOCKEY STORIES

YEAR

PAGE 42

Awards and Achievements:

Memorable Plays:

Funny Moments:

Quickfact: Did you know that about 450,000 young Canadians play organized hockey in Canada?

YEAR
TEAM

PAGE 43

NAME

AGE

HEIGHT

WEIGHT

POSITION

SHOOT/GLOVE HAND

NUMBER

COACH

ASSISTANT COACH

MANAGER

TRAINER

HOME ARENA

INSERT TEAM PHOTO HERE

PLAYERS IN BACK ROW

PLAYERS IN MIDDLE ROW

PLAYERS IN FRONT ROW

YEAR

DIVISION
LEAGUE

PAGE 44

TEAMS

#	Team	#	Team
1		7	
2		8	
3		9	
4		10	
5		11	
6		12	

EXHIBITION GAMES

			TEAM							PERSONAL							
NO	DATE	OPPONENT	SCORE		TEAM RECORD			GOALIE	GA	POINTS					TOTALS		
	MM/DD		US	OPP	W	L	T	TEAM PTS			G	A	PM	PTS	+/-	G	A	PM	PTS	+/-
01																				
02																				
03																				
04																				
05																				
06																				
07																				
08																				
09																				
10																				

REGULAR SEASON GAMES

			TEAM							PERSONAL							
NO	DATE	OPPONENT	SCORE		TEAM RECORD			GOALIE	GA	POINTS					TOTALS		
	MM/DD		US	OPP	W	L	T	TEAM PTS			G	A	PM	PTS	+/-	G	A	PM	PTS	+/-
01																				
02																				
03																				
04																				
05																				
06																				
07																				
08																				
09																				
10																				

Quickfact: Did you know that the first game broadcast over the radio was in 1923 from Toronto?

YEAR | **REGULAR SEASON GAMES** | PAGE 45

TEAM | PERSONAL

NO	DATE MM/DD	OPPONENT	SCORE US / OPP	TEAM RECORD W / L / T / TEAM PTS	GOALIE	GA	POINTS G / A / PM / PTS / +/-	TOTALS G / A / PM / PTS / +/-
11								
12								
13								
14								
15								
16								
17								
18								
19								
20								
21								
22								
23								
24								
25								
26								
27								
28								
29								
30								
31								
32								
33								
34								
35								
36								
37								
38								
39								
40								
41								
42								
43								
44								
45								
46								
47								
48								
49								
50								
51								

SEASON TOTALS

TEAM

GAMES	W	L	PTS	+/-

GOALIE

GAMES	GAA

PERSONAL

GAMES	W	L	PTS	+/-

Quickfact: Did you know that before 1911 there were nine players to a team?

YEAR

FINAL STANDINGS

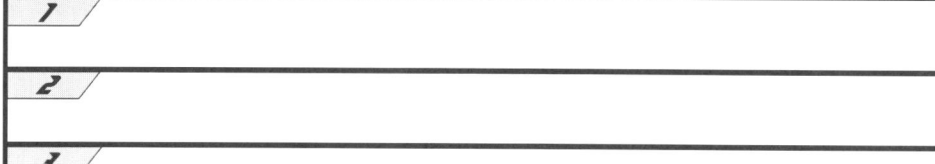

1.
2.
3.
4.
5.
6.
7.
8.
9.
10.
11.
12.

QUICK TIPS

- ☑ Drink plenty of fluids during the game to avoid dehydration which can lead to fatigue!

- ☑ Make sure you have the right curve in your stick because it can affect your shot and even the way you play the game!

- ☑ Do not wear new skates to play a game until you break them in well at practice or at home!

- ☑ Wear a good mouth guard as it will protect teeth, mouth, jaw and even the brain by absorbing and dissipating shock from a blow to the mouth or jaw.

- ☑ Your helmet should fit snugly and not wobble when you shake your head.

- ☑ The face guard/cage you wear should be attached securely to the helmet and should fit snugly to the chin.

Quickfact: Did you know that the number of players on the ice was reduced to six in 1911?

PLAYOFFS

YEAR:
PAGE: 47

SERIES 1

NO	DATE MM/DD	OPPONENT	SCORE US	SCORE OPP	W	L	T	SERIES RECORD W	L	T	TOTAL PTS	GOALIE	GA	G	A	PM	PTS	+/-	G	A	PM	PTS	+/-
01																							
02																							
03																							
04																							
05																							
06																							
07																							

TEAM / **PERSONAL** — **POINTS** / **TOTALS**

SERIES 2

NO	DATE MM/DD	OPPONENT	SCORE US	SCORE OPP	W	L	T	SERIES RECORD W	L	T	TOTAL PTS	GOALIE	GA	G	A	PM	PTS	+/-	G	A	PM	PTS	+/-
01																							
02																							
03																							
04																							
05																							
06																							
07																							

SERIES 3

NO	DATE MM/DD	OPPONENT	SCORE US	SCORE OPP	W	L	T	SERIES RECORD W	L	T	TOTAL PTS	GOALIE	GA	G	A	PM	PTS	+/-	G	A	PM	PTS	+/-
01																							
02																							
03																							
04																							
05																							
06																							
07																							

FINAL STANDINGS: _____

COMMENTS: _____
_____
_____
_____

Quickfact: Did you know that a McGill University player, named J.G.A. Creighton, was the first player to write down a set of rules for hockey in 1875?

TOURNAMENTS

YEAR

PAGE 48

TOURNAMENT NAME — DATE

NO	DATE MM/DD	OPPONENT	SCORE US	SCORE OPP	W	L	T	TEAM PTS	GOALIE	GA	G	A	PM	PTS	+/-	G	A	PM	PTS	+/-
01																				
02																				
03																				
04																				
05																				
06																				
07																				

Columns grouped under: TEAM RECORD, PERSONAL RECORDS (POINTS, TOTALS)

RESULTS:

TOURNAMENT NAME — DATE

NO	DATE MM/DD	OPPONENT	SCORE US	SCORE OPP	W	L	T	TEAM PTS	GOALIE	GA	G	A	PM	PTS	+/-	G	A	PM	PTS	+/-
01																				
02																				
03																				
04																				
05																				
06																				
07																				

RESULTS:

TOURNAMENT NAME — DATE

NO	DATE MM/DD	OPPONENT	SCORE US	SCORE OPP	W	L	T	TEAM PTS	GOALIE	GA	G	A	PM	PTS	+/-	G	A	PM	PTS	+/-
01																				
02																				
03																				
04																				
05																				
06																				
07																				

RESULTS:

Quickfact: Did you know that the game of hockey as we know it today was developed at McGill University in 1875?

YEAR

HOCKEY STORIES

PAGE
49

AWARDS AND ACHIEVEMENTS:

MEMORABLE PLAYS:

FUNNY MOMENTS:

Quickfact: Did you know that forward passing in hockey was allowed in 1918, making the game much faster?

YEAR
TEAM

PAGE 50

NAME

AGE

HEIGHT

WEIGHT

POSITION

SHOOT/GLOVE HAND

NUMBER

COACH

ASSISTANT COACH

MANAGER

TRAINER

HOME ARENA

INSERT TEAM PHOTO HERE

PLAYERS IN BACK ROW

PLAYERS IN MIDDLE ROW

PLAYERS IN FRONT ROW

DIVISION
LEAGUE

TEAMS

1	7
2	8
3	9
4	10
5	11
6	12

EXHIBITION GAMES

TEAM											PERSONAL									
NO	DATE	OPPONENT	SCORE		TEAM RECORD				GOALIE	GA	POINTS					TOTALS				
	MM/DD		US	OPP	W	L	T	TEAM PTS			G	A	PM	PTS	+/-	G	A	PM	PTS	+/-
01																				
02																				
03																				
04																				
05																				
06																				
07																				
08																				
09																				
10																				

REGULAR SEASON GAMES

TEAM											PERSONAL									
NO	DATE	OPPONENT	SCORE		TEAM RECORD				GOALIE	GA	POINTS					TOTALS				
	MM/DD		US	OPP	W	L	T	TEAM PTS			G	A	PM	PTS	+/-	G	A	PM	PTS	+/-
01																				
02																				
03																				
04																				
05																				
06																				
07																				
08																				
09																				
10																				

Quickfact: Did you know that goalie nets were introduced in 1900?

REGULAR SEASON GAMES

YEAR / PAGE 52

TEAM | PERSONAL

NO	DATE MM/DD	OPPONENT	SCORE US	SCORE OPP	W	L	T	TEAM PTS	GOALIE	GA	G	A	PM	PTS	+/-	G	A	PM	PTS	+/-
11																				
12																				
13																				
14																				
15																				
16																				
17																				
18																				
19																				
20																				
21																				
22																				
23																				
24																				
25																				
26																				
27																				
28																				
29																				
30																				
31																				
32																				
33																				
34																				
35																				
36																				
37																				
38																				
39																				
40																				
41																				
42																				
43																				
44																				
45																				
46																				
47																				
48																				
49																				
50																				
51																				

SEASON TOTALS

TEAM

GAMES	W	L	PTS	+/-

GOALIE

GAMES	GAA

PERSONAL

GAMES	W	L	PTS	+/-

Quickfact: Did you know that before goalie nets were used, two wooden poles were stuck in the ice marking the goal area?

FINAL STANDINGS

1.
2.
3.
4.
5.
6.
7.
8.
9.
10.
11.
12.

QUICK TIPS

- ☑ The hockey pants you wear should be comfortable and not restrict your normal skating movement.

- ☑ Make sure you dry your skate blades well after skating to keep them sharper and rust-free!

- ☑ Don't forget to bring plenty of tape for your stick and your equipment!

- ☑ Do not eat a heavy meal just before a game!

- ☑ Control of the puck means that the opponent cannot score.

- ☑ Do not criticize your goalie, instead support him for the next play!

Quickfact: Did you know that artificial ice first appeared in Canada in 1911?

PLAYOFFS

YEAR

PAGE 54

SERIES 1

NO	DATE MM/DD	OPPONENT	SCORE US	SCORE OPP	W	L	T	SERIES RECORD W	L	T	TOTAL PTS	GOALIE	GA	POINTS G	A	PM	PTS	+/-	TOTALS G	A	PM	PTS	+/-
01																							
02																								
03																								
04																								
05																								
06																								
07																								

SERIES 2

NO	DATE MM/DD	OPPONENT	SCORE US	SCORE OPP	W	L	T	SERIES RECORD W	L	T	TOTAL PTS	GOALIE	GA	POINTS G	A	PM	PTS	+/-	TOTALS G	A	PM	PTS	+/-
01																								
02																								
03																								
04																								
05																								
06																								
07																								

SERIES 3

NO	DATE MM/DD	OPPONENT	SCORE US	SCORE OPP	W	L	T	SERIES RECORD W	L	T	TOTAL PTS	GOALIE	GA	POINTS G	A	PM	PTS	+/-	TOTALS G	A	PM	PTS	+/-
01																								
02																								
03																								
04																								
05																								
06																								
07																								

FINAL STANDINGS: _____

COMMENTS: _____

Quickfact: Did you know that the Stanley Cup weighs about 37 pounds (17 kg)?

TOURNAMENTS

YEAR PAGE 55

TOURNAMENT NAME — DATE

NO	DATE MM/DD	OPPONENT	SCORE US	SCORE OPP	W	L	T	TEAM PTS	GOALIE	GA	G	A	PM	PTS	+/-	G	A	PM	PTS	+/-
01																				
02																				
03																				
04																				
05																				
06																				
07																				

Columns grouped under: TEAM RECORD (W/L/T/TEAM PTS), PERSONAL RECORDS — POINTS (G/A/PM/PTS/+/-), TOTALS (G/A/PM/PTS/+/-)

RESULTS:

TOURNAMENT NAME — DATE

NO	DATE MM/DD	OPPONENT	SCORE US	SCORE OPP	W	L	T	TEAM PTS	GOALIE	GA	G	A	PM	PTS	+/-	G	A	PM	PTS	+/-
01																				
02																				
03																				
04																				
05																				
06																				
07																				

RESULTS:

TOURNAMENT NAME — DATE

NO	DATE MM/DD	OPPONENT	SCORE US	SCORE OPP	W	L	T	TEAM PTS	GOALIE	GA	G	A	PM	PTS	+/-	G	A	PM	PTS	+/-
01																				
02																				
03																				
04																				
05																				
06																				
07																				

RESULTS:

Quickfact: Did you know that the original silver Stanley Cup was replaced by an exact replica in the mid-sixties to prevent further wear?

HOCKEY STORIES

YEAR
PAGE 56

AWARDS AND ACHIEVEMENTS:

MEMORABLE PLAYS:

FUNNY MOMENTS:

🏒 **Quickfact:** Did you know that tube skates were invented by a man named McCullough around 1905?